WHAT WAS ALL THE FUSS ABOUT?

Some other books by Daniel Weissbort

As Editor
POST-WAR RUSSIAN POETRY
THE POETRY OF SURVIVAL

Poetry
IN AN EMERGENCY
SOUNDINGS
LEASEHOLDER
FATHERS
INSCRIPTION
NIETZSCHE'S ATTACHÉ CASE

Daniel Weissbort

What Was All the Fuss About?

ANVIL PRESS POETRY

First published in 1998
by Anvil Press Poetry
Neptune House 70 Royal Hill London SE10 8RF

ISBN 0 85646 292 6

This book is published with financial assistance from
The Arts Council of England

Set in Monotype Janson by Anvil
Printed in Great Britain by The Cromwell Press Trowbridge

A catalogue record for this book is available from
The British Library

CONTENTS

127

II ODDS AND RULES

Note

The poems in the first section of this volume are drawn mostly from a number of short collections that were printed privately and sent to friends. These collections were themselves drawn from fairly copious notebooks kept between 1990 and 1997. Part Two draws on earlier notebooks and files; the earliest go back to the Seventies or a little before.

I should like to dedicate this collection to the memory of Joseph Brodsky who very flatteringly compared my work to that of Cavafy (very early in his career he translated Cavafy into Russian). On the other hand, he also told me once that life seems to have been my editor, by which I think he meant that I had no editor. I should also like to thank Ted Hughes, who urged me to 'publish' the little collections. This turned out to be an encouraging interim procedure.

D.W.

I

What Was All the Fuss About?

HYPOCHONDRIA

My body is giving me a hard time.
I'm for ever burrowing in health books
and counting imaginary woes.

Yet when I manage to put a foot forward
vistas open, at least for as far as you can see
without standing on your toes.

CAMBRIDGE AND ROME: A DREAM

Empire of memory, of the imagination,
with the ancient woman accompanying me
at once compliant and alert.
She knew the lingo, was impervious
to the mockery of the young,
the amateur taxi-driver, for instance,
who refused to take us from the high point to the coast,
because it was not his job.

And of the three ways down
unerringly I picked the one
that led directly to the city,
old and new mingling
in its day-filled thoroughfares
where my dark alley debouched.

ONCE AGAIN PEOPLE COME AND GO

Once again people come and go,
the police operate from without rather than within,
probably the secret service has not co-opted your neighbour.

The big, stupefying certainties
that rendered protest memorable
are no more.
     Nostalgia
waits in the wings.

HOME

I have steadfastly refused
to satisfy my unreasonable demands.
Had I attempted to do so
I'd not still be clinging to life.

But I have compromised,
achieved as much as could be hoped for
given the table's edge and a bruised sternum.

Perhaps my exile, too, will come to an end
and I shall return home.
After all, to say the least,
where I am is of no account
at any juncture in the history of the universe.

PARIS, 1953

The room smells of damp and *pourriture*.
The sink is antediluvian.
There's that engraving of Napoleon, his retreat from Moscow,
Bonaparte, a stubby figure in a sombre hat,
the buttons on his greatcoat still bright.
I am waiting for my friend to come back,
for him to tell me of his sexual adventures…

Oh, mother, mother,
no exiting into the long, long rue de Rennes,
Montparnasse one end, St Germain the other.

PRAGUE, 1968

My Czech friends have had it with all those big shots.

Castro, for one.
When I relayed Pablo's description:
'Fidel enters the room and...'
already they were shaking their heads.

They are shaking their heads now.
On Narodna, banner headlines:
BOBBY KENNEDY DEAD.
They tell me they are afraid.

'America... Oh, America...'

ONE FOR LENIN

The people is beguiled by music.
The people celebrates its commonality.
Does this also deaden the knout's pain?
Music, whether a lie or a great truth,
in soberer moments fails to entertain.

You are yourself not unaffected.
Those grand sounds enslave, or
you may provisionally accept that
Lenin's intolerance of music
was a point in his favour.

A FOOL RISES

I wake up. Yes!
All present and correct!
Alas, my body has not been rejuvenated
though, God knows, I tried,
plunging as deep as I knew how –
my ears are still ringing.

I haul myself out of bed,
tasks to perform.
The resolutions I might make
parade before my inner eye,
my outer eye clouded by
filaments and blobs.

I serve up breakfast –
porridge and coffee (two cups) –
and start constructing a future,
hoping things will work out.
The day moves sclerotically on its way,
I shuffle towards the morning post.

I shuffle towards the horizon.
An assembly is in session
but my concerns are not on the agenda.
What I have now may be all I'll ever have.
And yet, after that second cup,
I buckle on my briefcase.

THE NAME'S PROGRESS

At seven I was re-named Whitbord
by the headmaster of The Hall School, Hampstead.
It was 1942.

My actual surname, he explained,
was too German.

Weissbort, the name, was antipathetic.
Later, I surmised
it was a corruption of
Weissbart or Weissbrot –
these were no better.
For a while, though, I was Whitbord,
so very whinglish and whistleclean
that a continental, francophone mum-and-dad
scarcely disturbed my equanimity.

How did Mr Wathen light upon it?
My imagination falters. Perhaps, simply:
'We'll call him Whitbord.'
I doubt whether, properly speaking,
we were ever consulted...

All right, so he wasn't an anti-Semite,
at least not by the standards of those times...

Later, after the war,
Weissbort once again, I wondered why
my name had had to be changed.
But then, I often had to answer questions like:
Is that a German name?
No, in parentheses,
voiced or more usually unvoiced:
It's Jewish...

In England, they still occasionally ask,
in America never.
One reason to prefer America?

MOUCHES VOLANTES

Wherever I looked,
a shadow floated between.
And my eyeballs ached
following the *mouches volantes*.
I shall get used to this as well,
I told myself.

It's the same with Death.
A comfortable bed, warmth, enough food –
after all, what more could a man want,
as he approaches the nimbus of non-being?

COUNTING

He died two years after Suez, Hungary
and a decade before Warsaw Pact forces fucked Prague over.
World War Two was already thirteen years in the past
and he'd never told me what his thoughts were about the camps
in which most of the larger family perished.
But there were his daily quarrels at work with his brother, my
     uncle,
and there were his never-ending efforts to improve himself
or rather to turn himself into a competent *homme d'affaires*,
he who could still construe Virgil with ease
and knew his Bible in the original Hebrew, Aramaic, Greek.

What else?

It was my third year down from Cambridge, three up, three
     down,
my brother had already slipped over into his thirties,
mother was to remain as old as the century
for another twenty-seven years.

IN BETWEEN

In the late afternoon warmth
I pace back and forth on the beach.
No one, and for two hours more, no one.
But in between I lie on my side
trickling sand through my fingers.
I clear the surface around me of pebbles,
then probe for more beneath the surface.
I watch insects struggle up hill and down dale
and anthropomorphize idly.
When more purposeful thoughts press
I simply allow them to pass by
and then turn my attention to the waters,
wondering how loud they'd sound were I not so deaf.
I cup one ear, then uncup it.
Peace descends, the peace of a chamber
for sleeping in.

FORTUNATUS

I scrutinize the undergrowth for birds,
stare long at the sunset,
listen to the waters in their different moods.
Morning, and the fish-flies cling to the screen.
Unless I shake it, they'll stay there till they die.
A mass murderer, I sweep up the scintillating throng.

How fortunate I am that I can sit here unmolested, writing.
I've had more than my share of luck,
more than my share of being passed over.

EXECUTIVE

In this mask of mine only the eyes move
peering at that which draws near,
trying to see around corners.

I no longer hail my friends on the other side
since there is no help to be got from them.
In any case, how should I explain?

Instead, I improvise,
handling the bogeymen as best I can,
patting their behinds as they rocket past.

Sometimes I glance back.
But mostly I look ahead
to where the next comes barrelling along.

IMPRESSION

The *grand jeté en tournant*...
After thirty years, I still remember.
But that French girl in the black leotard
who preoccupied me then,
failed to impress.

WAVES

Too much like voices
that interrupt my reverie,
too much like talk,
like babble.

I keep flicking my eyes open
to make sure it's not people passing.
I cannot rest. The waves –
too much like garrulous people.

WHERE I AM

I sit here, quaking.
Also I keep nodding off.
My nose is cold, my palate itches,
I'm forever clenching my mutilated jaw.
But if I unclench it
a disagreeable sensation follows,
though what really concerns me then
is the scale of things.

Perhaps it's because
the whole of me comes into view
and I must re-imagine a death
that will encompass all of that.

THE SINGING TREE

When I pass the singing tree
the birds on the lower branches
climb its steps. If I pause
they go through the roof!
The tree's an evergreen,
the birds mostly common sparrows.
It's a plain old staging point
burning with song.

MARCH 1991

i.m. Paul Engle

We wait, breathless too,
ears pricked, as before an overture.
But nothing follows.
You'd think by now I'd have learnt!

Still, here's one won't just lumber off,
will argue long and acidly.

And behind the rumble of his death
I can hear him,
can even make out some of the words, choice…

Let 'em have it, Paul!

WHAT FOOLS!

To be a fool is also to be human.
Being human, you cannot but be a fool.
Yet who is to judge us, fools?
Who is to console us? Fools,
had you been otherwise
you'd not have been human.

God, least of all.
God remains on the sidelines.
God is judgment reserved.
God is that suspendedness
we sometimes call reality.

Fools! What fools!
Not that we did not possess the knowledge.

But our foolishness was stronger still,
and then it was too late.
It has always been too late for us Moseses,
though the Promised Land
is one we'd not have wished to enter anyway –
a land lit by a fearful dawn,
a gulag-land.

We, fools, in the last moment
glimpse eternity.

PAX AMERICANA

The barbarians were not so bad,
as much conquered as conquering.
But the new barbarians are irresistible.

What was precipitated
when the conscience-stricken found these shores,
fanning across the wilderness?

Here was Babel in reverse.
Here each proclaimed himself Human Being.
The arts lost their boundaries.

Meanwhile, in a convulsive effort to escape this embrace,
the world resurrected all its frontiers,
defending them to the death.

THE FRIDGE

At night, I hear it strumming,
the fridge, too fast.
I time it –
three to my one.

The cats are heaped,
slack, with ears.
I fill my lungs, listen to the outbreath
as the fridge throbs like a bomber.

FARM HOLIDAY NEAR POITIERS

After Sunday lunch, one of the brothers
would retire to the cellar
and drink home-brewed pear liquor.

That liquor was dry, like a cat's tongue.
And cats, there were several.
And other creatures too
in and out of the stone kitchen.
We listened to the crash of bottles
as he hurled the empties at rats.

Getting pissed and this sport
was the high point of his Sunday.

And why not?
I doubt if he ever hit anything save the wall.
It made the silence more tangible.

As for me, city boy, I'd retire,
lie on my bed with a tome of Conrad's sea tales,

while Jules (or was it Jerome?)
sprawled, propped against some sacks,
and heaved bottles at the shadows flying like cloaks.
Those crashes cleared the air.
A celebration, with explosions.

I balanced the great book on my belly
and brushed the spray from my brow.

WE ARE FULL OF HATRED

Full of hatred –
thank God we have enemies! –
we throw back our heads and howl.

The camera shows us open-mouthed,
shaking our fists at something, someone.

Those images, they are seductive.
People stare at them over breakfast,
fold the paper and go off to work.

MY WAR WOUND

Mr Macpherson lived in a dell with his daughter Vivian Van.
I don't remember a wife-and-mother.
Vivian Van was tall for her age.
Mac wore tweeds, smoked a pipe
and taught Vivian Van himself
so she didn't have to go to school.
A conscientious objector?
I don't know how I got to know them.
I could only have been six or seven, and even then

when I tried to recite 'Christopher Robin went hoppity-hoppity'
I forgot the lines. That was the first time, my birthday party.
    I think,
I think Vivian Van came to it.
Mac took me seriously, unlike some I might mention.
I had tea with him and Vivian Van after school
and he must have told me he didn't approve of school
and so he was giving Vivian Van her lessons himself.
Did I feel a little sorry for her,
a martyr to Mac's educational theories?
Of course, I wouldn't have put it that way.
Vivian Van hadn't much to say for herself.
Either she sat in a corner
or she was in and out of the room
carrying plates of sandwiches, cups of tea.
She was a big girl.

One day, during air-raid drill,
I fell and gashed myself above the lip.
I know this for sure because there's still a scar there –
my war wound, I call it.

SCOTLAND THE BRAVE

C was wounded in Korea,
after which he moved to Japan
where for a while he lived with a geisha girl
before returning to England
and then on to Cambridge.

That's where I met him.
I was fresh up from public school.
I remember with pleasure

his military braggadocio,
his leading us through dark streets, bawling
Scotland the Brave.

C was a philo-Semite
like General Wingate.
He plotted to help Israel in her plight.

Later he taught in a tough city school
and then went to Mexico.
Much later, I met him again.
He had a Mexican-Indian wife in tow.
He told me that the only hope for the world
was for the rich nations to accept lower living standards.

By now it was the Sixties.
Too late for me
but not for C.

1945

Conkers, the polish still on them,
remind me of that glorious moment
when, behind the cricket pavilion,
I found the earth strewn.
For once I was first on the scene.

Just before this I'd hit a six,
stepping forward, clouting the ball,
seeing it clear. Double figures!
For the first time I was into double figures!

And the war was over.

SIN: A DREAM

I was so busy confessing –
'His noble confession', you called it –
that we lost her.
At the exit to the store
I distracted you…
And then she was lost in the crowd.

I implored God,
so fraught that I woke myself up,
sweating, cursing, and lamenting
and at the same time assuring myself:
You've learnt a lesson
and there's no harm done
because it was just a dream.

And yet
for certain sins, though you wake,
there is no forgiveness either.

TOYTOWN USA

for Urszula Koziol

Our small Polish poet walks around toytown.
The eyes in her leathery face
are screwed up, so she seems to smile
or to be grimacing in pain.
She is going somewhere but keeps
fetching up against one wall or another.
Still, she is enjoying this ersatz freedom.

'Ça va, madame?'
'Ah, oui! Ça va très bien.

C'est agréable ici...'
She cocks her head,
no change of expression,
just that her cheeks are sucked in a little,
as if she were taking me into her confidence.
And I smile and nod, as if I understand.

BREAKING OF THE TABLETS: A DREAM

Was he my proxy,
seizing, when my head was turned,
the heavy slab of *cloisonné*
and dashing it to the ground?
'I did not believe in it'
he explained testily.
Then he spoke of a festival.
And he spoke, too, of Moses shattering
the Tablets of the Law.

His frown had been replaced
by a look of satisfaction.
Calmly he awaited the outcome.
I leaned over and examined one of the fragments.
The design seemed to lack aesthetic judgment,
though perhaps I could not tell,
so agitated was I.

And he? He did not accuse me
though I may have driven him to this deed
with all that loose talk of phoniness, of vulgarity.
He added, Cromwell-like, casting his eyes to heaven:
'I wanted to destroy something of His.'
So this was unquestionably his doing, not mine.
Yet oughtn't I to stand by him?

Then a man with a carrier bag appeared
and solicitously gathered up the pieces.
And I heard again the crack of the slab,
seized and dashed down, in an impulsive gesture
that shattered, too, the air of reverence.

TRIBES

The tribes are summoning their members:
'Come, all you who would make amends
for the sweet illicitness of mingling
for you know in your hearts that it was a sin!'
Priests are ringing bells,
jumping up and down in exultation
as the faithful respond to the call.
Every man spouts geo-political truths,
even the dumb are fluent now.
The leaders have borrowed their robes of office
from the museums of antiquities.
And scholars are hard at work
returning to the text books the incontrovertible facts.
There is a general air of festivity,
while men who never bore arms
learn the thrill of cradling weapons.
A sense of rightness suffuses all,
as if they were pursuing a destiny hitherto denied.
And now the marches must be settled
and those of mixed allegiances must make up their minds,
and finally the beatitudes are sung
over rivers flowing with blood.

MY GAME

In my mind, I'm still pulling on that gear.
And the ball, when you booted it right,
still registering its clarion call.
But my pal Johnny's off in some corner of the field
that'll be forever childhood.

When, by Lake Michigan,
I bowl a pebble overarm,
I seem finally to have learnt how.
Life turned out to be a super coach,
even if it also robbed me of my mates.

YOU LIE DOWN TO SLEEP

You lie down to sleep
with no one to kiss you goodnight
and within moments to abandon you there.

You lie on your side, one leg flung
across the entire width of the bed,
in the certainty that sleep is near.

You savor this certainty
like sweet, fresh water,
like being received in your saviour's arms.

SILENT FILM

A man sits in the garden
and listens to the buzz of all things;
mostly it's in his head, since he is rather deaf.

The man sits and listens.
And the pigeons coo faintly,
the wind approaches close enough to be heard.

The man feels rather than hears his scratching pen.
He looks down at what he has written.
And now he hears the grass growing
and the crackle of an ant's footsteps.
And he hears the whistling line of a spider.
Then he glances up and sees his wife's mouth open and shut.

STILL AT IT!

I've been scurrying about my city.
At ground level it hasn't changed much.
And when I get to where I'm going, I lift up my eyes –
there are generally enough familiar landmarks.

I'm growing old and I'm slow
but I can still occasionally manage a burst of speed –
that is, if my wits are about me,
if I'm not day-dreaming about the past.

I might drop dead, I tell myself.
But it seems to me that in that case
it would be someone else dropping dead.

TEMPORARY

We bob around, side by side.
Of course, once we've been picked up
this will come to an end.

Who wants to be reminded of such things:
grey seas, the cold, the odd speculative gull?
Meanwhile, though, we know each other as well
as only two people who have a common goal can.

IT'S TUESDAY AND THE GARBAGE MEN

It's Tuesday and the garbage men
are making their anarchic rounds.
The houses, for their part, are neutral.

I have slept three times:
planned two novels,
circled the globe,
resurrected several of the dead.

Something is scraping loudly now.
I hope it's on the roof and not under,
where my pen, too, scrapes.

AND NOW I'M FILLING IN QUESTIONNAIRES

And now I'm filling in questionnaires,
when all I wanted was the drama
and a part for me in it –
not answers.

MAKING SOMETHING OF IT

I paused, not overlong,
looked around, not overmuch.
It was as if the words
could not wait to present themselves.
So eager were they
they shoved one another aside.
I found room for them
but they kept switching places.
They were still at it years later.
But now when I give the signal
nothing much happens.
A few words might rise wearily
and start on the long journey,
but by the time they've arrived
all they can do is slump
into the places allotted them.
I have to send in the stretchers
to make something of it.

I BEAT MY FISTS AGAINST THE HOLLOW WALLS

I beat my fists against the hollow walls,
walls that whimper like sheet-metal.
Is this what always lay behind the wonder?
Is this the self I thought so rich and varied?

The illusion once dispelled
only simplicity remains.
I am not complex, I am simple,
art's been dispensed with.

This is the stuff of plain, joyless religions,
of a god who intended it so,
commanding us to love him.

I can only stare, both credulous and sceptical,
looking around at the congregation I am part of,
which has spent and overspent
its words of communion.

DECADES

Four decades since I first laid eyes on you.
Father had another year to live,
your mother was ten years younger than I am now,
a handsome woman, I remember her well –
that is, her youthfulness, her being
nel mezzo del cammin – and you,
a slip of a girl, with Audrey Hepburn looks.

Now I see you across the ranks, hands clasped,
standing beside your mother's grave.

Belly well out in front,
I make my way across to you,
before proceeding with you to my own mother's plot
at the far end of this gathering-in.

Living apart these two decades,
on separate continents even,
we offer one another
a certain companionship.
Our mothers, too, are still *mishpokhe.**

* *Yiddish: family*

WHAT OF DREAMS?

What of dreams? In the bewilderment
of waking, of looking around,
they deflate fast.

Where are you? I'm looking around.
England, America? If it's not one
it has to be the other.

And now the body makes its presence felt,
in case you've been wondering
or hoping –

the body, that bad news
there's no closing your ears to,
'least not in this life.

THE SECOND DAY: A DREAM

We passed the dread point
without fanfare. So
there was no looking back.
Once the other side
everything was new,
a bleakness.

A sense of relief succeeded that of loss.
What had been was a dream,
not unremembered, simply let go of:
'Easier this way.
Never thought I could, but I can.'

But what had happened to everybody,
those who remained behind,
those who left?

We heard small voices,
small but distinct –
our presence was amplified by them.
We saw our things drift off
like sea-weed on the tide.
We didn't care –
that was the point –
didn't care.

No sun shone, but it was day,
the second day.

BEACH

The gull jerks,
jumps back, wings uplifted.
I study the profile, the staring eye.
Shall I? No, non-interference.

The gull returns, stabs.
Leaps back. Returns. Stabs.
Thrash stab thrash stab...
I am invigorated by the spectacle!

The shallows are busy with small fry.
I wade, pebble-gazing.
The clear waters heave with nutriments.
The shoals sway, keeping their distance.

SON

My son gives good presents.
For instance, a fancy mirror,
a print of mediaeval Cambridge,
and when he was very young
a plastic contraption, like a miniature of organ pipes,
for holding pens and paper-clips.

These were not, as I first thought,
mere self-indulgences,
the proof being all were used,
all were absorbed.

Suddenly I remember that
I never brought my father any gifts.
Or have I forgotten?

In any case, what would I have given him?

Father? To decorate your room,
or something for your office wall?
Perhaps a god, a replica of whom:
Apollo, Zeus, Pallas Athene?
Or a bust of Racine, a print of Spinoza,
of Buber rather? Maybe books?

What did I know about you?
That you were well stocked with languages:
English, of course,
and Hebrew, Aramaic, Yiddish,
Greek, and Latin,
French, German…
Your library contained
in addition to books on accountancy and textiles
Homer, Virgil…
Sholem Aleikhem,

Vigny, Lamartine…
Romain Rolland, Anatole France…

My son gives good presents,
it's finally dawned on me,
after so many years of living with them.

What does he know, my son, that I never learnt?
What tongue does he speak,
out of what legacy that I forgot.

I'VE SETTLED FOR FRIENDSHIP ON WHATEVER TERMS

I've settled for friendship on whatever terms.
It is unprofitable to argue with necessity.
I didn't give myself enough credit before,
needing no encouragement to confess my wretchedness.

What I'd have taken for misunderstanding
I now gratefully accept as validation,
based on a provisional yet precise instinct.
We swap tall tales like there is no tomorrow.

SO, WHAT WAS ALL THE FUSS ABOUT?

'It's not so hard when you know how.'
But you always knew how.
It's not so hard when you realize that
of all the paths you might have taken
only one is left.

You peer at it
and as far as you can see

there's no obstacle, no impediment.
Instead, everything is surprisingly cheery
and there are still some to offer encouragement.

So, what was all the fuss about?

WE SPEAK OF INNER THINGS

We speak of inner things,
of us, of you, of I,
of what overnight has become obsolete.
Voice, having shaken off its listeners,
stands now bereft
even of these fickle audiences.
It can rehearse the rituals
or search in the sands
for small, strange forms,
seeds of future growth;
then, triumphant, wait
in full and foolish confidence.

THIS TALK OF MOTHER AND FATHER

This talk of mother and father
suggests unfinished business...

Well, at least it was begun?

I evoke them.
Has anything changed?
I scan the evidence –
photos, letters, household and personal effects –
like eavesdropping on them

or being a child again…
children eavesdrop
often with impunity.

So, I am a child again!
Still, I can handle it –
the irresponsibility
of a child's eavesdropping.

But I'm also keeping an eye on that child,
noting, analysing his feelings…

Here's one advantage of survival –
You get a second chance
to spy on your people,
running those films over in your mind.

Dreams supply a little topical action.

FREE AT LAST!

I look back,
not exactly to find answers,
but to check whether the dust has settled,
and, even if only provisionally,
to disengage.

And that's a big adventure,
probably the only one left.

Free at last!

For some, maybe all of life's like this.
For others, it's only near the end
that ties loosen enough.

But early or late, does it matter,
once you know that story
and have committed it to memory?

LEFT

They've left me behind.
I've stayed back with the language
that thought me disposed of,
a language blowing in the wind,
indifferent, oblivious.
I suppose it has done its job.
I suppose it's been decommissioned now.

Actually I like this aura
of everyone having gone somewhere else
and just the breeze pushing scraps around.
And maybe a few lesser scavengers.
And maybe an old fellow who,
since he can do nothing about it,
couldn't care less.

EACH TIME, IT'S A SORT OF KNELL

Each time, it's a sort of knell,
or perhaps a bell tolled by an idiot
who can't let go.

My language, too often exposed,
has little give in it,
though at least it is unashamed.

If I take off,
if I try to launch myself,
inevitably I ditch close by,
splosh around, then have to crawl
back onto the loathsome route.

It's hard even to pose the question:
What Is To Be Done?

What's to be done is
the same as it has always been.
But I'm a sort of rebel
who clings to his idleness,
going to great lengths to preserve it,
putting off to the last and even beyond
the inevitable surrender.

I'D LIKE TO TALK OF THIS AND THAT

I'd like to talk of this and that,
to write political poems,
poems about people, scenery, paradoxical situations,
poems about history.

But it seems that all I can do
is struggle to articulate the unrealized
and perhaps unrealizable.

I'm alluding to the preoccupation
with what I'm feeling,
what I'm feeling right now, for example,
about my continuing existence.

It seems that to define that feeling
is the least I can do.

Still, I've not given up hope
of one day managing,
and so being able to proceed
to what lie beyond the least –

my relationship to nature, the state, the collective past,
as well as the carnival of life.

HUMANITY: A DREAM

I dreamt I was being touched.
A small boy caught my eye,
then came over and ran his fingers
through my hair.

Must I be *in extremis*
for such to be unproblematic?
I dreamt that among the dewy young
I too sported a pure profile.

TRANSLATION

to a Russian poet

It is as if I had never left the room,
my head motionless, in place,
like some pre-Galilean planet.

PRESENCES

for Ruth

I am at one of two tables for two.
With a glass of red wine.
Facing the door.
A woman sits down at the vacant table.
Her back is to me
but soon she is joined by another woman
who faces but does not see me.
They talk in well-versed voices.

Close by, hands clasped behind his back,
legs apart, at ease
stands the chief waiter.
He advances to welcome guests,
again steps briskly forward to bid them farewell.

Each time, he returns to the same spot
and the same position.

I read the flyers I picked up at the Yves Klein exhibition
and remain pleasantly conscious of the chief
who keeps everything running like clockwork.

TIME SET ME DOWN HERE

Time set me down here.
Without preliminaries.
Can it be! I mean,
all those miles covered,
all those words, that smoke-screen?
And even the love maelstroms?
And the monuments raised?

Time set me down.
And what did I do?
I stayed put,
rocked back and forth,
hummed.

I hummed and didn't go anywhere.
Time watched, nudged me,
I rocked a little more.
But I didn't go anywhere.

After a while, time collected me,
took a few steps
and set me down again.
I trembled a little,
rocked from side to side.
Even though I looked dismayed
I did not leave the spot.

I did glance back though.
Everything was utterly unfamiliar.
Still, I didn't investigate.

Instead, I explored the idea of time
or thought of exploring the idea of time.
I had come so to dread its hand
it seems I was not able to –

only to note that without time's hand
this would never end.
Unless time got bored or exasperated
nothing would ever end.

FIFTY-NINE

He didn't quite make it,
staggered once, twice,
and was down.

Destiny, it had to be,
stood in the way.
It lashed out, flailed.
There was no getting by.

So, he never crossed over
from what was all contention
to tranquillity and gazing on vistas.

He never moved past
the roomful of quarrels,
the barterings and negotiations,
the plethora of objects.

He never took the crucial step,
leaving all that behind,
becoming aware of what may be
when suddenly all is permitted,
the prohibitions lifted,
the threats and judgments suspended.

For him, there was no sequel.

So, his spirit,
its tragic muteness,
has remained with me,
his sacrifice has ended at my feet.

He was consumed by age fifty-nine,
striving mightily to the very last.

TAKING HIS NAME

Always nothing follows.
But I persevere.
There's a moment's silence.

I do not believe in God or in Lords.
'Lord Krishna', say the Hindus.
I hate it!

No vestige should remain.
We are the only gods
(in lower case, of course).

But until our kingdom comes
and at the same time withers away
the risks could not be greater.

Some think this means
Armageddon is at hand.
It may be so.

VISITORS

Talk. Exchanging notes,
observations. Amusing
anecdotes. *Politesses.*
The occasional sharp rejoinder.
And then they go:
at the right time,
a little early,
a little late.

And silence, meaning
traffic on the A82,

wind in the trees,
the neighbour's car,
a dog, sheep.

I admit some words
but let few out.
The newspapers are upturned,
spilling their nectar.

Here I sit, in the stillness
preceding or accompanying pandemonium.
Time, like a meditating cat.
I sit here, motionless,
but there is no escape.

THE BUMBLE-BEE

I squint at a bumble-bee
in splendour passing over the eaves,
so full of itself, having survived
and been brought to perfection.

I imagine rapture as being its lot,
as all it is led to do
it does without hindrance now…

This now, which cannot be for me.

MASTER OF THE OBVIOUS

My Greek lover once said to me:
'You are a master of the obvious!'
But she exaggerated.

NOW

In my deafness
I still make out a burble of surf;
my eye caught by the glitter of leaves,
I imagine their murmur too.

This ought to be enough.
And yet for me it means
that I am waiting   .
for the gates to open –

for an invitation.

Do not be afraid! I tell myself.
Even at the eleventh hour,
you've all the time you need.

WHAT WAS I TRYING TO LEARN?

What was I trying to learn?
Leaves, wind, for instance,
and also the thoughts of men.

But above all, the rhythm,
eschewing both the giver and the given,
out of what foolishness, what pride.

Yet I think neither. It was
as if I were undone,
something maybe of memory not applied

so I could not begin.
I did not begin. Instead
I put on disguises, preened,

despaired, and yet continued to think
the sound would be heard all through,
the wave at last descend upon the shore.

MY COUNTRY

My country?
What is my country?
It never spoke to me,
assuming all was well.

But all was not well.
I didn't know,
didn't and still don't,
though I wait,
hopeful as ever.

In England I was born.
Anticipation was my lot.

THEN AND NOW

From birth to death
the spirit has little time to unfold
or room to spread its wings.
Already, having learnt some skills,
you sit, imprisoned in wisdom and impotence,
a mite ahead of those that come to you
for solace or advice.
Your words need not travel far
to be seized upon now,
transformed, enshrined even.
Your self, left to its own devices,

dreams or glances back
over the short distance
separating then from now.

WHAT WE ARE A PART OF

What did not surface,
so as to expose an angle or a tip, a peak,
but on which, instead, my gaze focused
gave out an admonitory hum, a signal.

I bore myself, one among many,
in this Roman Triumph
with a god out front.
I didn't hang on. No room
with the sky that colour,
rain, or sun, or the wind,
the low clouds, earth-bound.

It was always with us, the poor world,
poetry, what we are a part of,
pity, impermanence the clue.
And our gods, straw simulacra.
And the pride. How
did we come to believe or know?

Flesh begins here, at the tip of the finger.
It is a sea that clots, a note sustained,
silence of before, but particularly of after,
the sum of all those afters.

VISION EVER WAS INWARDNESS

Vision ever was inwardness.
The flat earth couldn't afford it,
even tucking out of sight
as it did, so cranes might head
on, up and over, coming at us
with their thrust, their rusty calls
and wings like the doom of blankets.

Steppes, right there,
as if deposited and no place to go,
this being the last shore
where the horde gathers
heavy with weaponry,
the attack never coming.

SEA SIGNALLED IN THE AIR

Sea signalled in the air
above the salt marshes.
Pools were here, drops, shards
from the shattering
of a mind. The cows,
gatherers, strayed.
Along the dikes came pilgrims
shouting Te Deums
that touched neither god nor beast.

REACHING

His hand, reaching
to the armpit, clutched
sand, drew it forth.
He propped his chin on the edge
and, magnifying the grains,
cast his eyes upward,
while his fingers still fluttered
in the moistness.

It was thus far and no further,
so all that remained
was to get to his knees, to his feet,
arms folded now
as if in resignation
or satisfaction.

What remained was
only worlds to conquer,
empires to build.
He held the pain of that fumbling
folded, and silken-skinned
stood like Bonaparte.

DUCKS AND DRAKES

The ducks, oblivious of us, seek out and mate.
The drake pads about her as she grazes,
as far from him in spirit, so it seems,
as we're from them, observing this
annual exchange. Oh, do not pry!
Do not eavesdrop on them, though their world
ignore you, like the heavenly kingdom
visible only to the mind's eye.

SLEEPING WITH ONE'S GREENGROCER: A DREAM

The kippers descended from the top shelf
to the accompaniment of a lecture on the dangers of
    smoking.
Did I know... And did I know...
Wrapping them with a deliberate lack of expertise,
all the while fixing me with a disapproving eye.

I walked away, clutching the poorly wrapped kippers
and beat a path between shelves of food
in this improvised supermarket,
eventually catching up with the women.

I do not quite recall the context
but now it is with surprise
that I hear my elderly female cousin
say of her greengrocer
matter-of-factly and quite distinctly:

'If you sleep with them...'

IT IS IN MY POWER NOW

It is in my power now
not to put a foot wrong,

though I still do
out of boredom –

or not so much boredom
as curiosity,

as you might hold a mirror up
to a corpse's lips.

STILL THERE

Still there –
when I open my mouth –
my hateful voice,
as when you open your eyes
and you've still got cancer.

Still there –
with its baggage,
its monogrammed cases,
waiting confidently
for the limousine to pull up.

ALEWIVES

The lake renders its silver.
A few gulls feed fitfully.
I walk about in the stink,
searching for a little freshness.

I am thinking about life and death.
Those tiny flies that infiltrate on warm, still nights,
the daddy-long-legs, feeling its way like a blind man.
And the birds: sailing gulls, circling buzzards,
sandpipers on twinkling legs.
And you, doing whatever you are doing,
thinking whatever you are thinking…

And myself walking here,
an adolescent in his seventh decade,
picking his way between dead fish, the alewives,
peering at them from time to time,
the heads especially, those eye-sockets.

Teeming life, teeming death,
and my life come to this,
which is all right. 'It is all right'
I do not have to tell myself.

'I do not have to tell myself!'
I tell myself in wonder
and dismay that it has come to this.

THE HARDNESS BENEATH

I spread the towel,
lie on the hard sand.
I stare at the sky,
at that cloud, not moving –
like a seahorse, hippocampus –
moving quite swiftly now
as if released by my naming it.
And another, another,
all of them on the move.

Then gulls –
the long, thin wings with a kink in them
slowly fanning or held,
gull upon gull,
in the apparent stillness.

I lie on the hard sand and mutter:
Is this a rehearsal?
But what a relief anyway
with the hardness beneath,
to stretch out here rather than be balancing
on the two narrow soles of my feet.

THE GLAD CHILL

It wasn't death I met head on
or only in a manner of speaking,
since what I encountered had no head.
It brought me up sharp though,
took my breath away, as visions will,
except it wasn't a vision either.

Rather it was like a sheet of metal
which might have reflected me, except I had no reflection,
or hadn't got the nerve to really look.
It brought me up sharp
blocking my way forward
so that I turned around and sideways on,
superstitiously marking time, miming,
as I expressed what I can only describe as
a glad chill.

For an instant, I grasped the reality of my imminent
    non-being,
and either then or just before
of my being as the one experiencing this.
And there was regret, too,
as I thought of all those who no longer were
and who are disembodiedly still alive within me.

I see them more as imps that have hitched a lift.
In dreams they can be reconstituted
and a sort of conversation with them is struck up
or at least remains a perpetual possibility.
Except, of course, that it isn't with them…
But, then, we know about that.

A glad chill? I said.
For one reason, because I know that…
In short, I was brought up short

and looked around,
or practised looking around
for as yet I saw nothing.
I turned my head here and there,
breathing loudly,
as you might in a dark room,
getting your bearings.

EASY DOES IT!

I've always been in a hurry.
Like a Hasid
running to keep an appointment
with God maybe,
or to conclude a deal,
or just not to be any place long.

Envy does it better.
A cinch, you're not worth bagging.
Wherever you're going you've already arrived.

I consider language.
I consider the road that drifts past
like clouds seen from an airplane.
I consider the muscles
that prop me up if I'm careful.

Is this old age?

I consider my life, my contemporaries.
I consider writing letters to them.
I write letters,
crossing out, crossing out.

Is this depression?

I consider resistance,
involvement, play-acting.

I consider going to India.
Would maidens bathe in my stillness?
Would words finally let me be?

BORN AGAIN

Language begins to strike poses.
I watch uneasily.
Was it for this I let go?
I take a deep breath, look around me.
O, if only the landscape were bleak,
with seas seen through a veil,
and this held, until a day
clear of all others
descended upon us!

Some resort to technical or scientific jargon.
Used correctly this impresses,
giving its users confidence.
Others admit colloquialisms –
one at a time.

For instance, they might chat with God.
Unrhyming *terza rima* appeals to many –
or paragraphs of *vers libre*.
Meanwhile, the sniping continues.
Occasionally, as the generations pass
there are encomia for the recently deceased.
Often, as well, for the long unread.

The editors keep a stern eye on it all,
with magisterial pronouncements taking stock
and pithily highlighting the poor prose of this verse.
We are back at school
where the grammarians in charge
chide us, ironize, and appoint prefects.

We are back where we must vie
for prizes, accolades,
playing the game,
complaisantly uninventive, unrebellious,
keeping within bounds that parody boundlessness.

Language stops dead…
I stare at it –
whatever its condition
in that moment of arrested movement
it lets itself be stared at,
not trying to hide.
We wait.

Then, deliberately, we release it, very slowly.
It proceeds, its eye on us and not on where it's going,
gathering speed but continuing to fix us.
Recruited by this gaze
we jog along,
laying the line as we go,
sowing the scenery.

But there is a larger dream or reverie,
a dark and wordless chamber,
a place of renewal?
Leaving, we look around.
It is as if we had been cast up on a desert island,
or in another age.
What happened to the others?

Do not ask!
Their voices will soon be heard,
that travelling show of chatterers
will appear over the pristine horizon.

Take care lest you conjure it up.
Pay attention, rather,
to the words being born again.

II

Odds and Rules

GROUND RULES

Take a Jew
who is spat upon,
around whom little children gather
and make pipi.

Not hard to find?

So, all right,
set him down in New York City
or the Golden West,
or somewhere in between.

What do you have?

One who need no longer put up with
indignities and humiliations.
He brushes himself off
and for a generation or so
refuses to be overwhelmed
by nostalgia.

KILL: A DREAM

The little English boys
in prep-school uniforms
interrupted the lecture
to ask if there was a mouse.
They dispatched one of their number to look under the rock,
while the others positioned themselves close
to drive out whatever the creature might be,
a mouse, for instance.
And indeed a large mouse did show itself
and at the very entrance to the cave was confronted by

a startled rabbit, which batted it
several times about the head.
'The rabbit,' I observed loudly,
remembering that rabbits possessed stout claws,
'is finishing it off.' The mouse
managed to crawl on a certain distance
and then keeled over,
and one of the cats –
the boys by then had metamorphosed into cats –
strolled across to look.
I knew instantly it could not be dead
if only because rabbits do not prey on mice.
Besides, it was not a mouse but a rabbit now
lay on its side with staring eye,
the cat nudging, nuzzling underneath.
And as we watched –
how could we not watch! –
it bit into the rabbit's throat,
so we presumed.
There was a pause in the proceedings
and then the rabbit,
as we had all along suspected it might do,
wailed like an infant,
its eyes filmed over
and its head sank back.
And the cat pressed down upon it, that supine head,
as you might squeeze air out of a balloon,
except it was blood spurted from a puncture hole.
Then the cat smeared the blood over the rabbit's head,
caressing, anointing it.

SOLD

The house was sold
and a sign appeared
and then was taken down,
because the youngest objected:
'The first thing I'm going to do when I grow up
is buy it back...'

THE CHILDREN GREW TIRED OF WAITING

The children grew tired of waiting.
They dispersed.
'So soon?' I told myself,
there being no one else left.

I let my arms fall.
Perhaps it was all a dream?
In any case
I was no more ready to meet my maker.

WINTER

A pale light on the rooftops.
Leafless twigs, bony fingers,
one spinach-coloured crown.
These are what I see from my bed.

A squirrel, flicking its tail,
jerks along the power line.
A bird speeds past, distracting me.
Another trips across the pitch of the roof

like an escaping prisoner, a bug.
And speaking of bugs, this morning
there were none left.

THE POET

The poet swings through words.
He's not to know where he is going
but words don't let him down
if he keeps reaching for the next.

O, but he *does* know when it's over.
Something catches his eye –
a bright book-jacket.

INTRODUCING F.R.: A DREAM

for Jon Silkin

… always that first encounter with
unidentifiable violence.
Then I wake, vowing: No more sleep!
I shall not enter again that charnel house!

But I know it's behind me.
Now these characters simply use my slumber to congregate in,
to be together yet apart in,
I being the host nobody recognizes.
Like last night…

It was a grand reception, Jewish style.
I buttonholed a famous pal, a touring poet:
'Who'd pay to listen to me?' I said

to him who had himself already turned away.
After that, we were shown to our places
at the head table, yet a little to one side.
Already seated in the middle was D.S.,
the well known MP and former cabinet minister.
'Isn't that D.S.?' I observed.
You nodded: 'Yes.'
But then I myself was not so sure.
It was our wedding feast,
my second and your first.
Mother had returned to organize the celebrations,
but now not for her friends who, like her, were mostly dead,
rather for my would-be ones,
those jackals that earlier had torn my flesh.
I speculated: anonymity was well advised, and yet –
what of the groom's obligatory speech!

The problem was not resolved
since I awoke before being called upon.
I awoke, leaving that crowd to its own devices,
awoke, an oration forming in my mind
to introduce… to introduce…
F.R., the celebrated poet, passing through.

WITNESSES

to Claude Lanzman

He asks questions. Mostly
people are eager to talk.
They even vie with one another.
His questions are simple enough –

where they were,
what time it was,
how long it took…

Questions like these
you can answer.

MONTEVIDEO

for David Ross

1

In Cherry Hinton we got talking to
an old salt who told us of his travels.
One port-of-call had been
Montevideo… Montevideo!
He urged us to see the world –
and why not, when
before the post office, we noticed
an ancient bicycle for sale,
a tandem, reasonably priced.

2

After the drinking,
litres of young red wine,
we set out from the port of Bordeaux,
crossed a bridge, headed inland
through dusty suburbs. Then
grape arbours, vineyards. We joked:
Perhaps we'd just keep going,
and what a shame we didn't have that bike
we might have bought in Cherry Hinton.

DIARY OF A CHAMBERMAID

La petite Claire collects snails in the forest.
Madame asks the *curé* if she might
help our her 'virile' husband
with certain... gestures... since
ça fait mal... she cannot...
He dreams of huge molluscs
like old-fashioned chamber-pots.
but they are to be dispatched with two blows,
one to the brow, the other to the underside.

He has a metal hammer for it.

One to the brow, the mollusc ceases to move.
And then the *coup de grâce.* Oh,
but they are such mild creatures,
so vulnerable in their eyeless fluttering...

SUN

He was the leader of my gym team
though I was his senior.
I didn't particularly like him
but liking wasn't the issue.

I would stare, trying to solve this conundrum
but didn't find the words, either rare or humdrum.
So, I simply endured wordlessly.

His last name was Cryer.
For me the name signified light
or more particularly an aureole of fire.

SUNDAY MORNING

The ducks are at it again,
one pair straight ahead of me,
two more males standing by
as though awaiting their turn.
I circumnavigate them.

All day yesterday it rained.
Today the sun shines, the vistas
misting between branches.
On the river path, by the little chapel
all is action, noisy chases, captures.
The Lord, too, makes a grab for me
as I pass his singing house.

VARIATION ON A CLASSIC SCI-FI THEME: A DREAM

I void a cargo of packages, small sarcophagi.
Some have come undone, the rest
are neatly stacked in the back of the truck,
their ranks filling it to the roof.
A deceased population, desiccate, unodoriferous.

Relieved of these dead ones, these carcasses,
I rise again, who'd protested the indignity,
the rude intervention, imagining I held within,
barely contained, a reeking world,
not this sanitized battalion.

MR WATHEN'S DEMISE

When in wartime the prep-school head changed my Jewish
    surname
because it sounded German,
we did not question his decision.

That headmaster has long since met his end.
His next-in-line but two or three
pointed to the old man's full-length portrait
and told me how this happened.

Mr W raised his brolly and strode
confidently into the Finchley Road.

Like Moses crossing the Red Sea, I thought.

THE JACKET POTATO

i.m. Rachel Ojalvo

The jacket potato that fell into my palms
inscribed itself on my memory.
It was baked by Mrs Ojalvo, my best friend's mum,
who lived on the first floor of our block of flats
and dropped it into my waiting hands.

She died far away, in São Paolo, Brazil,
much younger than I am now.
By the time I learnt of this
she'd been dead many years.

Can I say that nothing tasted so good again?
Yes, but that's not the point! What mattered more
was her leaning on the windowsill,

her small face, the expression on it, contemplative and –
if this is not too plangent –
concerned.

SOAP OPERA

I'm trapped in a Soap.
Of course, it isn't really.
I'm not listening to anyone,
not to nature,
not even to *my* nature.
Besides, my right heel aches
and won't permit it.
A nerve, enfleshed,
flashes calf,
the backs of knees.
A kind of deep fatigue follows.
Nature cannot compete
and so I dread waking,
even if sleep's no boon.
I wake into such bleakness
that any good it may still have done
is forfeited at once.
And then I thumb my heel,
find the exact spot,
exert some pressure,
until my toes tingle.
Then, maybe, the phone rings,
sounding out distances.
I consult my calendar,
strap on my foot-armour,
drink two, maybe three cups of coffee.
And now my thigh is tingling.
I walk slowly, trying not to limp,
but my belly is distended:

A diet, if you please, a diet!
Meanwhile, the Soap waits patiently
for me to take my place in the action.
Only the dead can be consulted
and they've their own problems.

ROYAL COMMAND PERFORMANCE

We know what's expected,
to stand when she enters,
sit once she's seated.
In her presence
differences are at once resolved
and we unite in loyal applause
which she acknowledges. Always she
is what we expect,
and we what she expects.

SNOW ZONE

I'm in a snow zone.
Whatever is happening elsewhere
here snow's the thing.

You don't have to think about it.
A mindless process
like being digested.

Nevertheless, one glances up at the birds
that cross and re-cross.
Or maybe they are breaking out.

BIRDS

A flock of birds, starlings or grackles,
a flock of crosses, like a skewed cemetery,
tilting, slithering, as if a hand rocked it.
Then they are drawn back into the trees.

Bare branches, dark with sentinels.
I stop for a moment and the air shudders with their rising.
If instead they were to mount an attack
in moments they'd strip me to the bone.

THE CASTLE: A DREAM

The path to the castle bisects
a corner of the narrow cemetery strip
over from the church.
I'd a few moments to spare
and strolled across to take a look
at what I'd passed so often
but not till now found time to visit.
Beyond the turnstile
a landscape seemed to stretch,
although I knew this couldn't be.
Still, the illusion of a certain loveliness persisted
and yet the path, the graveyard once traversed,
became a narrow, rocky road,
curving between walls that rose on either side,
ending abruptly in a chamber
of crumbling stone, open to the sky.
Ledges permitted me to scramble to the top
but on the other side I found another chamber,
larger and with no means of scaling it.
I turned and started to retrace my steps
and suddenly noticed, on my left,

another chamber which I had missed before.
This one was roofed, a sort of storeroom,
for in it benches, pews and wooden thrones
were heaped like props on top of one another.
There was a window, set high in the wall,
towards which I began to climb.
But when I'd neared the summit,
on which a park bench trembled,
I lost heart... I forgot to mention
that all this while
a kind of ecclesiastic music played,
just as, before this, I realized now,
someone had been whispering to me on the path.
Hurrying, I clambered down again, and in the doorway met
new visitors. I nodded to them,
relieved they had not caught me in the act.

BAG LADY

That old lady
hauling her pneumatic plastic sacks,
snarling when someone has the cheek
to ask can he help her cross the street,
was something in the Resistance.
Was? Isn't she still?

MY FURRY FRIEND

My furry friend
sits on the arm of my chair.
He sits with folded paws,
gazing over the brink.
Then a sound turns his head,

light catches his eyes
and he lifts himself,
routinely stretches,
thuds to the floor,
stands.

He ambles off in the direction he is pointing.
Before he knows it
he is eating again,
or staring at his dish.

What follows is a puzzle.
He just stands.
That's when he seems least animal,
most like me.

FRUSTRATION

I have been telling them for years
And they are sick of my telling them
But they still haven't heard!

I'd been telling them for years
And they were sick of my telling them
So I stopped and they asked me:
What was it you were saying?

Then I told them again
And didn't add: But I've already told you.
And they listened to me for the first time
And I was happy.

Soon, though, I grew despondent
Only too soon I grew despondent
Could it be that this was all I had to tell them?

LO, MORNING!

I emerged from my dreams
as from a dark cloud.
Didn't look back.

I rubbed my eyes,
Aladdin's lamp.

Lo, morning!

THE EXECUTION: A DREAM

Last night they executed two,
a man and a woman. Poets.
We were strung out along the catwalk
above the place of execution
to voice our protest.
A well-known younger poet,
a friend of theirs, was to address us –
there was even talk of
obstructing the course of justice.
Presently the prisoners, smiling, joking,
were led in.
First they appeared among us,
then below, where a small crowd gathered.
Journalists?
As the moment approached
some bowed their heads.
I laid my own on the iron railings and crooned.
The young poet began:
'It gives me no pleasure…'
I was confident he'd find the words.
'So, if she'd not got an apartment…'
This was about the woman, a negress.

There was some laughter.
Wonderful, I thought,
how he's managed to strike just the right note.
They're so good at this, such pros!
Meanwhile final preparations were being made.
I caught sight, over the heads of watchers –
I had abandoned my place by the rails –
of a single marksman, adjusting his earpads,
while the condemned couple was seated
at the end of what was a kind of gallery.
In a clear voice the man asked for a cigarette.
(He made the most of this opportunity to show his courage.)
Then there was an indeterminate rattle.
Overheard
two marshals reassuring someone that
the end was instantaneous.
Also, something about
the bullet having only to brush the victim for...
Hearing no more, I imagined a kind of detonator.
And glancing down now,
saw that already the people were dispersing.
Two journalists pointed their cameras
for a close-up, presumably, of blood on the ground.
And I recalled newspaper pics
which might have been of anything,
rain, spilt milk, a weird shadow.
But I also thought:
If these don't turn out well,
no doubt the archives will furnish them with better ones.

FEELINGS LAST LONGER

Yesterday, at a play which ended
with the problematical suicide of the main character,
a man at odds with society although true to himself,

I remembered with satisfaction
all the writing I had done.
A smile tugged at my features.

Naturally I surrendered to this feeling,
not expecting it to last.
At the same time I considered –
obliquely, absently –
the dilemma powerfully enacted in the play.

In this agreeable state
I further recalled a visit to the Tate Gallery
where, at the Rothko exhibition,
I had concluded that while there's life
there is no reason creativity should cease.
This, in connection with Rothko's suicide.

Today as I walked about,
I realized I was glad to be
where, as a young married man, I had briefly lived.
Now, back here but on my own,
it was as if I had never left.
And the happiness, it lingered.

STALLED: A DREAM

They were negotiated
and not without pleasure…
In any case, I don't remember.
But finally came the guileful one.
A descent it was –
generally, I should have said –
at first no harder than the rest,
so I'd time to fret about my clothes,
my pristine new coat,

smudged, not tattered yet, but smudged.
O, and there were three of us
and then a fourth.
He passed, impatient with me.
And someone said, '… jumped'.
But when I looked, expecting to see him limp away,
there was this sheer drop of fifty feet onto the rocks.
We were on a tilting platform, concrete,
itself set on stilts.
Peering over and around, I saw
that these were held in place by wooden props
only the rules decreed must brace it.
So, as I shifted my weight,
the platform, too, moved.
The three of us pressed our bodies to it,
hugging it as best we could.
I looked up. Above was a field,
a ridge that seemed negotiable,
though where it led was uncertain –
no doubt, away from the path we cleaved to now,
which must return us to the valley of our origins.
Moreover, so oblique was the platform,
I did not think we'd make it to the ridge.
It was clear though that we had to try,
if we were to save ourselves, must circumvent this peril
laid up for us by a malevolent djinn.
Meanwhile we remained there.
We could neither unthink the dread predicament
nor imagine how the fourth had escaped.
We stayed, knowing that whatever happened
we would be left behind.
Salvation there might be, but not for us,
condemned, like Simeon Stylites, to this roost,
longing for terra firma,
above us or below.

MONET'S 'LE PRINTEMPS'

At first I thought the painting was of light –
a man, a woman, borderless.
But then, against my better judgment,
I concluded that *listening* was the subject.
Either he's talking, while she listens,
her face half-turned away,
or she's absorbed by what she herself is saying
while he, gazing at her, listens docilely.

The trees of the orchard,
dark trunks spiralling,
listen too. Beyond, an emphatic sky
eavesdrops through the blossoming boughs.

THE KHAKI RIVER SCINTILLATES

The khaki river scintillates.
On juicy, bluegreen banks
yellowbrown fronds salaam.
Shall I submit to this charge of light and warmth?

'You must! You must!'
But I do not surrender.
The mad race we call summer is on
and I gather my strength to go the distance.

THE FOOD DRUM

from an Igbo folktale

Innumerable invisible hands of ancestors
urge and coax fruit from the earth,
summon food from the air.
This is what the drum accomplishes.
They cannot but serve when the drum sounds.
Its voice towers above the drummer,
spreads all about him,
plunges far below,
rousing the great serpent.
As if by magic
he may pluck the fruit even as it grows;
even as he stretches out his hand
fruit grows into it,
tipping its head.
Soon he has eaten his fill.

The next time he beats the drum
the sound again spreads like a cloud
and penetrates beneath the earth,
so he feels the ground tremble;
but now, as from behind closed doors,
seven ancestors spring forward
and whip him and belabour him
and pick him up and fling him down
and trample on him and shake him
and then leave him for dead
lying under the stars,
the drum on its side next to him.
But he feels cleansed by this beating,
satiated by it too.
Aching all over
he picks up the drum and wonders
which is the right side and which the wrong.

THE PRESS AT A REHEARSAL OF
THE LONDON SCHOOLS SYMPHONY ORCHESTRA

Like scavengers they circle this earnest flock
from whose fixed expressions
music lifts.

HAIKU

I look up from work
birds are squabbling
above the peonies.

SPRING

Foliage, the tint of baby's shit,
fuzzes the trees, and in it
darker nodes, like flies.
Spring! A bad cold's my response.
Last night, Ravi Shankar performed,
not at *his* best either.
But there were moments,
when he got in over his head
and had to find his way out again...
He didn't take much notice of us then.

The trees, of course, take not the slightest notice of us.
This upsurge simply happens,
skeletal shapes camouflaged rather than transformed,
though the young trees are lucent,
the blossoms about to embark
on their short trip from an alert inwardness
to an indifferent drop from the single staring eye.

I thought I'd write of the sea,
that the sight of it, the feel
of the wind off it, the rank smell of it
were enough a part of me. But now,
exhausted, sweaty after a toilsome night,
with something awful, something tragic weighing on me,
the sea's recoiled. Indeed,
what I might summon seems
not unrelated to the unnamed horror
that has seized me. Perhaps it was already there.
Perhaps it was reckless
to admit those several impressions.
Now nothing is recoverable
that would not render this situation even worse,
though I regret the apparent freedom
from all mundane concerns and errors,
the mind planing above garrulous waves,
concentration and that kind of flight, of hovering
over, even beyond the swell,
like a perpetual in-breath, lifting me up,
depositing me in a snug home, a veritable crow's nest
where at last I open my eyes
to all the seas, rising to greet me.
Yes! I regret it!
But it comes after, before
what I must first grasp
and what I cannot, shall not be able to,
even if I talk endlessly, like the waves,
hoping to entice, to precipitate a morsel of meaning,
maintaining an air of expectancy,
ready to pounce on whatever shows itself.
Nothing does! Nothing is redeemed.
Or perhaps a certain joy begins to wake,
to revive, to look about it,
yesterday, preparing to vault the night and its monsters

that can perhaps be left to themselves —
being given an airing was enough! —
and re-establish itself this side
of an abyss whose precipitousness is postponed.
And yet when I consider this joy closely
I see there are more problems to be solved,
more gates to be propped open,
each of which stubbornly resists
so that, as usual, I search for
a quicker exit, an easier escape.

SEASIDE IMAGES

A child draws the soles of his feet
over slick sands. Hair fluttering
he smiles at his surfing shadow.

*

Khaki-and-rust
smokes through the waters
sweeping to the horizon.

*

Wavelets bubbling.
Limp, pearly crab-claws.
Clover-gutted jelly fish.

*

Phosphorescent moss.
Subcutaneous blue
the sun's hand brittle on the waters.

*

Breakwater in its loud bath
foam greasing its flanks
fingering the trapped pools.

*

On the opalescent shore
seagulls shuffle their wings...

THE STORYTELLER

Who are you that rub your eyes
outside the cinema at four in the afternoon?
Work, man, you are the storyteller!

THE OWL

with baleful eyes operated from within
transmits electronic hoots.

THE GARDEN

The nettles are tall and proud
and I look in vain for the four-leaved clover
by the swing with its mossy seat.
But birdcalls echo, as though blessing her
that she permitted this riot, this rankness.
The white rabbit nibbles here all day,
shining, as our white cat once did,
which only the morning dapple hid.
The laburnum is gone, the cherry, the acacia.

But the two hawthorn trees, white and red,
straggle high.
Humus mounts in the wrecked shed.
Rusted toys and tools lie
undisturbed in this stillness where
even now I have a ringside seat.

ODDS

'Very few people die of this type of cancer,'
said the young dentist, as we followed the path
to the otolaryngology clinic.
'You'll be all right,
without any question of a doubt.'

'Question of a doubt'?
It struck me as unidiomatic
or rather a case of mixed idioms.
But then I was in America. Anyway
his words did the trick, kept me going for decades.

At the same time, no one had ever spoken to me
of my death: very few people die!
The first unmistakeable encounter with what
before I had only imagined I knew
when I witnessed, even if at closest quarters,
my father's last exhalation.

But the bright-faced young dentist wanted to convince me
that the odds, for the time being,
were still in my favour.
And he did.

I.M. M.M.

Today your chin creases,
your face puckers, and I think –
surely this is a joke, though in bad taste!
We'll deal with it, my friend,
as we've dealt with all such *conneries*...
But now it's the nurses speak your name,
which for them sums up
the history of your illness.
Their greetings convey a soberer truth
than our exchanges in that lovely world
of impetuous beginnings.

SOON

The bluffs are rusty with fall foliage,
more and more trees come clean.
A sense of accomplishment fills me, as I note
how many didn't make it, trees and folk.

For the first time, I start to relax.
Soon the snows will come.

I'm in good shape.
I throw back my shoulders,
puff out my chest.

Soon the snows will come!
Soon the snows will come!

IT LOOKED AS IF

It looked as if her will to live
had persuaded death to let her be,
she would always get away with it.

Of course she didn't. But she lay
so fiercely, furiously lifeless, that it seemed
even now death must be having second thoughts.

ARCHAEOLOGY: A DREAM

For two nights I've been digging.
Trying to disinter mother?
Trying to clear away the snow?
That I do not want to wake before it's done
is all I know.

How time passes
when you're having fun!
Stuffed animals, tools
on a shelf in the German blockhouse,
a metal elephant, a gun.

I'd been playing at guns.
On the shelf, now, the identical one,
lacking only a firing pin.
I pick it up, peer down the barrel,
see light at the other end.

If I wanted to, I could take it with me.
But we're all adults here.
And we know this object is worthless,
no longer an instrument of glory.
Had we been kids
it would have been another story.

COLLECTING YOU

My stomach turns as I think of the empty flat
stripped of all, even its floor covering.
I hope you are not wandering still
behind the familiar front door, wondering why
nobody comes, and I close my eyes,
trying to get a grip on myself.
But what I'm on the edge of draws me.
I am trying to reverse time, to show
that I can return at will,
recovering what I need.

And what do I find?
Remembered smudges, scratches, the creak
of a cupboard door,
views from the windows.
I sit on the bare boards –
there's nowhere else to sit –
and note the marks where pieces stood,
for instance, the boudoir grand,
and then the light patch on the wall
left by the large cubist painting –
a bible scene, three kings,
worshipping a wooden image...

And now I know why I've returned.
It is to collect you,
to take you from this place.
I summon you from all of your rooms,
from all the corners, cupboards and closets.
And sitting there cross-legged, I hug my belly,
hug it, like the Satsuma Buddha
that squatted impassively on the canteen,
under the still life of onions and parsnips.

A HOME FOR CANCER

Cancer does not so much lie in ambush
as wait for the way to be made straight,
a comfy home made ready, a nest.
And this home must be just right
before cancer will consent to be a guest.
Cancer is discriminating.
It will not put up with second best.
It inspects the premises carefully
and if anything's not up to scratch
returns to its waiting post.

EVEN DEAD, MOTHER, YOU'RE A SIGHT SANER

Even dead, mother, you're a sight saner
than the rest of us! When I look back
it seems like cooler weather then.
Your level gaze, your chic attire,
the way you held yourself.

Now the lid is off,
the vegetation's running riot,
all sense of proportion has fled.
The call of the wild
finds me scribbling helplessly.

OUT OF BOUNDS

Like a slow insect, a plane
etches a path over my window pane.
Today there is no sun, and yet already
heat rises through the cracked soil
to contaminate the atmosphere.

I woke late for the birds –
besides, the fan, much like the surf itself,
subsumes other sounds.
A breeze touches my face and forearm
and I stare anxiously at the innocuous world
beyond the pale.

I'M SURROUNDED BY SILENCES AND ABSENCES

I'm surrounded by silences and absences.
Last words and sights mark time
as gingerly I detach myself from them.
It's better this way. This way
they can get on with their lives.

LOST

He looked about him.
In what direction should he set off?
He did not want to move
from where he had been left.
But people were staring.
He had to go.

New and Recent Poetry from Anvil

Peter Dale
EDGE TO EDGE
New and Selected Poems

Dick Davis
TOUCHWOOD

Michael Hamburger
LATE

James Harpur
THE MONK'S DREAM

Donald Justice
ORPHEUS HESITATED BESIDE THE BLACK RIVER
New and Selected Poems

Peter Levi
REED MUSIC

Thomas McCarthy
THE LOST PROVINCE

Stanley Moss
ASLEEP IN THE GARDEN
New and Selected Poems

Dennis O'Driscoll
QUALITY TIME

Sally Purcell
FOSSIL UNICORN

Peter Russell
THE ELEGIES OF QUINTILIUS

Ruth Silcock
A WONDERFUL VIEW OF THE SEA

Ken Smith & Matthew Sweeney (eds.)
BEYOND BEDLAM
Poems Written Out of Mental Distress